meatballs

meatballs

30 recipes for mouthwatering variations

First published in 2011
LOVE FOOD is an imprint of Parragon Books Ltd

Parragon
Queen Street House
4 Queen Street
Bath BA1 1HE, UK

ISBN: 978-1-4454-2876-5

Printed in China

Introduction written by Christine France
Additional recipes written by Christine France
Cover and additional internal photography by Clive Bozzard-Hill
Home economy and food styling by Valarie Barratt

Notes for the Reader
This book uses imperial, metric, and US cup measurements. Follow the same
units of measurement throughout; do not mix imperial and metric. All spoon
measurements are level: teaspoons are assumed to be 5 ml, and tablespoons are
assumed to be 15 ml. Unless otherwise stated, milk is assumed to be whole, eggs
and individual vegetables, such as potatoes, are medium, and pepper is freshly
ground black pepper.

The times given are an approximate guide only. Preparation times differ according
to the techniques used by different people and the cooking times may also
vary from those given as a result of the type of oven used. Optional ingredients,
variations, or serving suggestions have not been included in the calculations.

Recipes using raw or very lightly cooked eggs should be avoided by infants, the
elderly, pregnant women, convalescents, and anyone with a chronic condition.
Pregnant and breast-feeding women are advised to avoid eating peanuts and
peanut products. People with nut allergies should be aware that some of the
prepared ingredients used in the recipes in this book may contain nuts. Always
check the packaging before use.

Contents

What is a meatball?

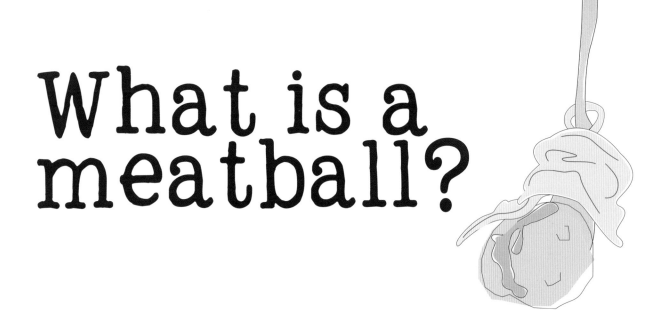

A meatball can be just about anything that can be ground and ends up round! Meatballs are not just for spaghetti, so be adventurous and try them in other ways, too.

Almost every nation has its own variation on the meatball theme, many making use of different meats and flavor additions, such as herbs and spices, from spicy Middle Eastern koftas to the more delicate Northern European frikadeller (flat, pan-fried dumplings of ground meat).

Perhaps the reason meatballs are so popular is that they are economical and very easy to make. They're also endlessly versatile, and can be the base for quick, nourishing family suppers or party dishes, soups, packed lunches, sandwiches, or canapés.

Meatballs can be fried, broiled, braised, poached, steamed, baked, or microwaved.

Which meat to choose?

Meatballs can be made with any good-quality meat that can be ground: beef, pork, ham, bacon, lamb, turkey, chicken, or even game.

When shopping for meat to use for meatballs, remember that it's not always the expensive cuts, such as beef tenderloin, pork tenderloin, or chicken breasts, that are best because they can be too low in fat. Instead, choose one of the cheaper cuts that tend to have slightly more fat to help make moist, flavorful meatballs.

When buying prepared ground meats, don't be tempted to buy the cheapest ground available. It can be very fatty, which will not only make your meatballs too greasy but much of the fat will be released from the meat and the meatballs will shrink.

Some meats, such as chicken, are not widely available in ground form. If you don't have a meat grinder at home, a food processor can do the job. Use the "pulse" button to

avoid overprocessing, because it's important to retain some texture and not reduce the meat to mush. In the case of chicken, the thigh meat is the best choice for tasty, moist meatballs.

Not just meat

Seafood, including fish fillets and even shellfish, can be made into tasty fish balls, too. Even vegetarians needn't miss out, since all kinds of vegetables and legumes can be used as a base for veggie balls.

Texture enhancers

Bread or breadcrumbs, either white or whole wheat, are often added to meatballs as a binder, and they also create a softer consistency. The bread can be soaked in water or milk first, but be careful not to add too much liquid or the meatballs will be too soft.

Other grains, such as rice, oats, cornmeal, or cracker crumbs can be used in the same way as bread and are a useful extender for the meat when you're on a budget.

Seeds or nuts add a delicious crunch to simple meatballs, either added to the mix or used as a coating.

Moisture givers

The amount of moisture needed in meatballs depends on the cooking method. For threading onto skewers or for frying, keep the mixture fairly firm, because soft, wet mixtures will lose their shape or fall apart. More moist mixtures are best cooked in a sauce or baked in the oven.

Some meatball mixtures are bound with beaten egg to keep the ingredients firmly together, or simply enriched with egg yolk. Grated cheese, or finely chopped vegetables—onions being the most popular—will add moisture as well as pepping up the color, texture, and flavor. Try raw grated carrots, zucchini, or beet for a change.

Flavor boosters

Meatballs can be spiced up with almost anything that comes to mind. If you like spicy food, try adding chile flakes or chili sauce, or for a more subtle, warm spice, use a little curry powder or paste, or ground cumin, coriander, or cinnamon.

Herbs are the perfect flavor addition to meatballs, either fresh or dried. The most useful to keep in your pantry are parsley, thyme, cilantro, chives, and rosemary.

A dash of Worcestershire sauce, ketchup, or mustard can add a zip to a plain meatball mix in seconds.

And don't forget the salt and freshly ground black pepper—if you're not sure how much to add, fry a small amount of the mixture in a little oil so you can taste to check the seasoning before cooking the rest.

Top tips

- Choose good-quality ground meat with not too much fat.

- Make sure all your meatballs are the same size, so they cook evenly.

- Use a small ice-cream scoop to portion out the mixture for rolling into balls. Tiny ones can be scooped with a melon baller.

- For most purposes, the perfect size of a meatball is about 1½–2 inches/4–5 cm in diameter; larger ones are difficult to cook evenly unless in a sauce. Meatballs for canapés are usually smaller, bite-size mouthfuls.

- Your hands are the best tool for shaping meatballs. Roll the mixture between your palms to get a firm, round shape every time.

- Lightly wet your hands when shaping to prevent soft mixtures from sticking.

- If the meatballs will be shallow-fried, coat lightly in flour or fine breadcrumbs to form a crust on the outside.

- When time allows, it helps to chill the meatballs for at least 10 minutes before cooking to allow for the texture to firm up slightly and for the flavors to combine.

- A wok makes a good cooking pot for frying meatballs because they can be moved around easily without breaking up.

- Use a couple of palette knives or spatulas instead of tongs to turn the meatballs when cooking to prevent the mixture from breaking up.

- Drain off any excess fat from fried meatballs by placing onto absorbent paper towels before adding to sauces or serving plain.

Freezing

Meatballs are perfect for freezing, so if you're making a batch of meatballs, it's worth making a double quantity to keep for another day.

Shape the meatballs as usual and freeze uncovered on a baking sheet; or cook first, then cool completely before freezing. When frozen solid, the meatballs can be transferred into sealed plastic bags or freezer containers for storage.

Most types of meatball can be frozen successfully for 3–4 months, but if the recipe contains garlic, freeze for only 1 month before use.

To use, thaw overnight in the refrigerator before cooking or reheating. To cook from frozen, add extra cooking time and test to make sure the meatballs are thoroughly cooked.

Saucy

spaghetti & meatballs

serves 4

1 tbsp olive oil

1 small onion, finely chopped

2 garlic cloves, finely chopped

2 fresh thyme sprigs,
finely chopped

1 lb 7 oz/650 g ground beef

½ cup fresh breadcrumbs

1 egg, lightly beaten

1 lb/450 g dried spaghetti

salt and pepper

sauce

1 onion, cut into wedges

3 red bell peppers, halved and
seeded

14 oz/400 g canned chopped
tomatoes

1 bay leaf

Heat the oil in a skillet. Add the chopped onion and garlic and cook over low heat for 5 minutes, until softened. Remove from the heat and put the mixture into a bowl with the thyme, ground beef, breadcrumbs, and egg. Season to taste with salt and pepper, then mix well. Shape into 20 meatballs.

Heat a large nonstick skillet over low–medium heat. Add the meatballs and cook, stirring gently and turning frequently, for 15 minutes, until lightly browned all over.

Meanwhile, preheat the broiler. To make the sauce, put the onion wedges and bell pepper halves, skin-side up, on a broiler rack and cook under the preheated broiler, turning frequently, for 10 minutes, until the bell pepper skins are blistered and charred. Put the bell peppers into a plastic bag, tie the top, and let cool. Set the onion wedges aside.

Peel off the bell pepper skins. Coarsely chop the flesh and put it into a food processor or blender with the onion wedges and tomatoes. Process to a smooth paste and season to taste with salt and pepper. Pour into a pan, add the bay leaf, and bring to a boil. Reduce the heat and simmer, stirring occasionally, for 10 minutes. Remove and discard the bay leaf.

Meanwhile, bring a large pan of salted water to a boil. Add the spaghetti, bring back to a boil, and cook for 10 minutes, or according to the package directions, until tender but still firm to the bite. Drain the spaghetti and serve immediately with the meatballs and sauce.

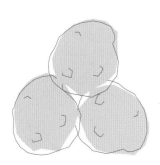

meatballs in almond sauce

serves 6-8

2 slices white bread, crusts removed

3 tbsp water

1 lb/450 g freshly ground pork

1 large onion, chopped

1 garlic clove, crushed

2 tbsp chopped fresh parsley plus extra to garnish

1 egg, beaten

freshly grated nutmeg

all-purpose flour, to coat

2 tbsp olive oil

lemon juice, to taste

salt and pepper

almond sauce

2 tbsp olive oil

1 slice white bread

scant 1 cup blanched almonds

2 garlic cloves, finely chopped

⅔ cup dry white wine

1¾ cups vegetable stock

To prepare the meatballs, place the bread in a bowl, then add the water and let soak for 5 minutes. With your hands, squeeze out the water and return the bread to a dry bowl. Add the ground pork, onion, garlic, parsley, and egg, then season with grated nutmeg and a little salt and pepper. Knead the ingredients well to form a smooth mixture.

Spread some flour on a plate. With floured hands, shape the meat mixture into about 30 equal-size balls, then roll each meatball in flour until coated. Heat the oil in a large, heavy-bottom skillet. Add the meatballs, in batches, and cook for 4–5 minutes. Using a slotted spoon, remove the meatballs from the skillet and reserve.

To make the sauce, heat the olive oil in the same skillet in which the meatballs were fried. Break the bread into pieces, add to the skillet with the almonds, and cook gently, stirring, until the bread and almonds are golden brown. Add the garlic and fry for an additional 30 seconds, then pour in the wine and boil for 1–2 minutes. Season to taste with salt and pepper and let cool slightly. Transfer to a food processor. Pour in the vegetable stock and process the mixture until smooth. Return the sauce to the skillet.

Carefully add the meatballs to the almond sauce and simmer for 25 minutes, or until the meatballs are tender. Taste the sauce and season with salt and pepper, if necessary.

Transfer to a warmed serving dish, then add a squeeze of lemon juice to taste and sprinkle with chopped parsley. Serve immediately.

meatballs with cracked olives

serves 6

2 slices day-old bread, crusts removed

3 tbsp water

9 oz/250 g lean fresh ground pork

9 oz/250 g lean fresh ground lamb

2 small onions, finely chopped

3 garlic cloves, crushed

1 tsp ground cumin

1 tsp ground coriander

1 egg, lightly beaten

flour, for dusting

3 tbsp olive oil

14 oz/400 g canned chopped tomatoes

5 tbsp dry sherry or red wine

pinch of hot or sweet smoked paprika

pinch of sugar

6 oz/175 g cracked green olives in extra virgin olive oil

salt

Put the bread in a bowl, add the water, and let soak for 30 minutes. Using your hands, squeeze out as much of the water as possible from the bread and put the bread in a clean bowl.

Add the pork, lamb, 1 chopped onion, 2 crushed garlic cloves, the cumin, coriander, and egg to the bread. Season to taste with salt and, using your hands, mix together well. Dust a plate or baking sheet with flour. Using floured hands, roll the mixture into 30 equal-size, small balls, put on the plate or baking sheet, and roll lightly in the flour.

Heat 2 tablespoons of the oil in a large skillet, add the meatballs, in batches to avoid overcrowding, and cook over a medium heat, turning frequently, for 8–10 minutes, until golden brown on all sides and firm. Remove with a slotted spoon and set aside.

Heat the remaining oil in the skillet, add the remaining onion, and cook, stirring occasionally, for 5 minutes, or until softened but not browned. Add the remaining garlic and cook, stirring, for 30 seconds. Add the tomatoes and their juices, sherry, paprika, and sugar and season to taste with salt. Bring to a boil, then reduce the heat and simmer for 10 minutes.

Using a handheld mixer, blend the tomato mixture until smooth. Alternatively, turn the tomato mixture into a food processor or blender and process until smooth. Return the sauce to the saucepan.

Carefully return the meatballs to the skillet and add the olives. Simmer gently for 20 minutes, or until the meatballs are tender.

swedish meatballs

serves 4

2 potatoes, cut into chunks

½ cup fresh breadcrumbs

1 lb 7 oz/650 g ground beef

1 small onion, grated

1 egg, lightly beaten

1 tsp brown sugar

pinch each of grated nutmeg,
ground allspice, ground ginger,
and ground cloves

¾ cup fine dry breadcrumbs

6 tbsp butter

salt and pepper

sauce

2 tbsp all-purpose flour

1 cup beef stock

1 cup heavy cream

Cook the potatoes in a pan of salted boiling water for 20–25 minutes, until tender but not falling apart. Drain, put into a bowl, mash well, and let cool slightly.

Add the fresh breadcrumbs, ground beef, onion, egg, sugar, and spices to the bowl. Season to taste with salt and pepper and mix well until thoroughly combined. Shape the mixture into walnut-size balls, rolling them between the palms of your hands. Roll the meatballs in the dry breadcrumbs until thoroughly coated.

Melt the butter in a large skillet. Add the meatballs, in batches, and cook over medium heat, stirring and turning occasionally, for 10 minutes, until golden brown all over and cooked through. Remove with a slotted spoon, drain on paper towels, and keep warm while you cook the remaining batches.

When all the meatballs have been cooked, keep them warm while you make the sauce. Stir the flour into the skillet and cook, stirring continuously, for 1 minute. Remove the skillet from the heat and gradually stir in the stock, then add the cream. Season to taste with salt and pepper, return the skillet to low heat, and cook, stirring continuously, until thickened and smooth.

Return the meatballs to the skillet and simmer for 10 minutes. Serve immediately.

meatballs in red wine sauce

serves 4

2 cups white breadcrumbs

⅔ cup milk

12 shallots, chopped

2 lb/900g ground beef

1 tsp paprika

1 lb/450 g dried tagliatelle

salt and pepper

fresh basil sprig, to garnish

red wine sauce

2 tbsp butter

½ cup olive oil

3 cups sliced wild mushrooms

¼ cup whole wheat flour

scant 1 cup beef stock

⅔ cup red wine

4 tomatoes, peeled and chopped

1 tbsp tomato paste

1 tsp brown sugar

1 tbsp finely chopped fresh basil

Put the breadcrumbs into a bowl and pour over the milk. Let soak for 30 minutes.

To make the sauce, heat half the butter and half the oil in a pan over low heat. Add the mushrooms and cook for 4 minutes. Stir in the flour and cook for 2 minutes. Add the stock and wine and cook for 15 minutes. Add the tomatoes, tomato paste, sugar, and basil. Season to taste with salt and pepper and cook for 30 minutes.

Preheat the oven to 350°F/180°C. Mix the shallots, beef, and paprika with the breadcrumbs and season to taste with salt and pepper. Shape into 12 meatballs.

Heat the remaining oil and the remaining butter in a skillet. Add the meatballs and cook until browned. Transfer to a casserole dish, pour over the sauce, cover, and cook in the preheated oven for 30 minutes.

Bring a large pan of lightly salted water to a boil over medium heat. Add the pasta and cook for 8–10 minutes, or according to the package directions, until tender but still firm to the bite. Drain and transfer to a serving dish. Remove the casserole from the oven and pour the meatballs and sauce alongside the pasta. Garnish with a basil sprig and serve immediately.

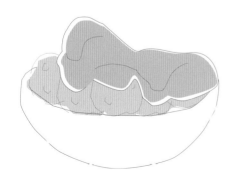

spicy meatball risotto

serves 4

1 thick slice white bread, crusts removed

water or milk, for soaking

1 lb/450 g fresh ground pork

2 garlic cloves, very finely chopped

1 tbsp finely chopped onion

1 tsp black peppercorns, lightly crushed

pinch of salt

1 egg

corn oil, for pan-frying

14 oz/400 g canned chopped tomatoes

1 tbsp tomato paste

1 tsp dried oregano

1 tsp fennel seeds

pinch of sugar

4 cups beef stock

1 tbsp olive oil

3 tbsp butter

1 small onion, finely chopped

scant 1½ cups risotto rice

⅔ cup red wine

pepper

fresh basil leaves, to garnish

Soak the bread in the water for 5 minutes to soften. Drain to remove all the liquid. Mix the bread, pork, garlic, onion, crushed peppercorns, and salt together in a bowl. Add the egg and mix well. Form the mixture into 12 even-size balls.

Heat the corn oil in a skillet over medium heat. Add the meatballs and cook through. Remove and drain.

Combine the tomatoes, tomato paste, herbs, and sugar in a heavy-bottom pan. Add the meatballs and bring to a boil. Reduce the heat and simmer for 30 minutes.

To make the risotto, bring the stock to a boil in a pan, then reduce the heat and keep simmering gently over low heat while you are cooking the risotto.

Meanwhile, heat the olive oil with 2 tablespoons of the butter in a deep pan until the butter has melted. Stir in the onion and cook for 5 minutes, until golden.

Reduce the heat, add the rice, and mix to coat in oil and butter. Cook, stirring continuously, for 2–3 minutes, or until the grains are translucent.

Add the wine and cook, stirring continuously until reduced. Gradually add the simmering stock. Stir continuously and add more liquid as the rice absorbs each addition. Increase the heat so that the liquid bubbles. Cook for 20 minutes. Season to taste.

Lift out the cooked meatballs and add to the risotto. Remove the risotto from the heat and add the remaining butter. Mix well. Arrange the risotto and a few meatballs among 4 plates. Drizzle with the tomato sauce, garnish with the basil, and serve.

turkey meatballs with pasta

serves 4

12 oz/350 g ground turkey

1 small garlic clove, finely chopped

2 tbsp finely chopped fresh parsley

1 egg, lightly beaten

all-purpose flour, for dusting

3 tbsp olive oil

1 onion, finely chopped

1 celery stalk, finely chopped

1 carrot, finely chopped

14 oz/400 g canned tomatoes, strained

1 fresh rosemary sprig

1 bay leaf

12 oz/350 g dried penne (pasta quills)

salt and pepper

freshly grated Parmesan cheese, to serve

Put the turkey, garlic, and parsley in a bowl and mix well. Stir in the egg and season to taste with salt and pepper. Dust your hands lightly with flour and shape the mixture into walnut-size balls between your palms. Lightly dust each meatball with flour.

Heat the olive oil in a pan. Add the onion, celery, and carrot and cook over low heat, stirring occasionally, for 5 minutes, until softened. Increase the heat to medium, add the meatballs, and cook, turning frequently, for 8–10 minutes, until golden brown all over.

Pour in the strained canned tomatoes, add the rosemary and bay leaf, season to taste with salt and pepper, and bring to a boil. Lower the heat, cover, and simmer gently, stirring occasionally, for 40–45 minutes. Remove and discard the herbs.

Shortly before the meatballs are ready, bring a large pan of salted water to a boil. Add the pasta, bring back to a boil, and cook for 8–10 minutes, or according to the package directions, until tender but still firm to the bite. Drain and add to the pan with the meatballs. Stir gently and heat through briefly, then spoon onto individual warmed plates. Sprinkle generously with Parmesan and serve immediately.

soup with meatballs

serves 4-6

5 dried mushrooms

12 oz/350 g ground beef

1 onion, finely chopped

1 garlic clove, finely chopped

1 tbsp cornstarch

1 egg, lightly beaten

3¾ cups beef stock

½ cup watercress, stalks removed

3 scallions, finely chopped

1–1½ tbsp soy sauce

Put the mushrooms into a bowl and pour in warm water to cover. Let soak for 15 minutes, then drain and squeeze dry. Discard the stalks and thinly slice the caps.

Mix together the ground beef, onion, garlic, cornstarch, and egg in a bowl until thoroughly combined. Shape the mixture into small balls, drop them into a bowl of ice water, and let stand for 15 minutes.

Pour the stock into a large pan and bring to a boil. Drain the meatballs well, add to the pan, and bring back to a boil. Reduce the heat and simmer for 10 minutes. Add the mushrooms, watercress, scallions, and soy sauce to taste and simmer for an additional 2 minutes. Transfer to serving bowls and serve immediately.

Skewered

greek-style kabobs

serves 4

1 lb/450 g lean, finely ground lamb

1 medium onion

1 garlic clove, crushed

½ cup fresh white or brown breadcrumbs

1 tbsp chopped fresh mint

1 tbsp chopped fresh parsley

salt and pepper

1 egg, beaten

olive oil, for brushing

warmed pita and salad, to serve

Preheat the broiler to medium. Put the ground lamb in a bowl. Grate in the onion, then add the garlic, breadcrumbs, mint, and parsley. Season well, with salt and pepper. Mix the ingredients well then add the beaten egg and mix to bind the mixture together. Alternatively, mix the ingredients in a food processor.

With damp hands, form the mixture into 16 small balls and thread onto 4 flat metal skewers. Lightly oil a broiler pan and brush the meatballs with oil.

Cook the meatballs for 10 minutes, turning frequently, and brushing with more oil if necessary, until browned. Serve the meatballs tucked into warmed pita with salad.

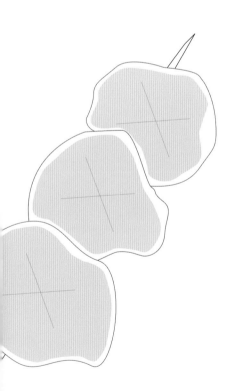

beef & lamb skewers

serves 4-6

8 oz/225 g fresh ground beef

4 oz/115 g fresh ground lamb

½ onion, grated

2 tbsp chopped fresh
flat-leaf parsley

1 tbsp chopped fresh cilantro

1 garlic clove, very finely chopped

1 tsp ground cumin

¼ tsp ground cinnamon

½ tsp hot paprika, or to taste

½ tsp harissa paste, or to taste

½ tsp salt

pinch of cayenne pepper,
or to taste

olive oil, for brushing

chopped fresh mint, to garnish

mixed salad and warmed pita,
to serve

Put the ground meat in a food processor and process to a paste. Add the onion, herbs, garlic, cumin, cinnamon, paprika, harissa paste, salt, and cayenne pepper and process again until blended.

Wet your hands and roll the mixture into 12 equal-size balls. Lightly brush 3–4 long, metal skewers with olive oil. Press one meatball around one skewer and squeeze the 2 sides together to seal, then roll it back and forth in your palms to form an oblong "sausage" about 4 inches/10 cm long. Add 2 or 3 more meatballs to the skewer, depending on its length, and shape in the same way. Repeat with the remaining skewers. Cover with plastic wrap and chill in the refrigerator for at least 1 hour, but ideally up to 4 hours.

Preheat the broiler to high. Brush the meatballs with a little oil and cook under the broiler, turning frequently for 8–10 minutes, or until cooked through.

Using a folded cloth to protect your fingers, hold the top of each skewer and use a fork to push the meatballs off. Serve with a mixed salad and warmed pita.

lamb skewers

serves 4

12 oz/350 g lean ground lamb

1 small onion, finely chopped

2 tsp each ground coriander, ground cumin, and paprika

1 tbsp chopped fresh cilantro

2 tbsp chopped fresh mint

3 tbsp olive oil

generous ⅓ cup plain yogurt

2½–inch-/5-cm piece cucumber, grated

2 tsp mint sauce

4 cups mixed leaf and herb salad

1 tbsp lemon juice

salt and pepper

Put 8 wooden skewers into a shallow bowl of cold water and let soak for 30 minutes. Put the lamb, onion, spices, cilantro, and mint into a food processor with plenty of salt and pepper. Process for 1–2 minutes, until finely ground. Transfer to a bowl, cover, and chill in the refrigerator for 30 minutes.

Preheat the broiler to high. Divide the mixture into 8 golf ball-size balls. Wet your hands and shape the meatball around the skewer, forming a sausagelike shape. Brush with a little of the oil and cook under the broiler, turning frequently, for 15–20 minutes, until cooked through.

Meanwhile, combine the yogurt, cucumber, and mint sauce in a small bowl and season with salt and pepper.

Put the salad greens into a large bowl. Whisk the rest of the oil with the lemon juice and season to taste. Pour the dressing over the salad greens and toss to coat. Serve on or off the skewers, with the salad and cucumber-and-mint yogurt.

chicken kabobs

serves 4-6

⅓ cup raw cashew nuts

2 tbsp light cream

1 egg

1 lb/450 g skinless, boneless chicken breasts, coarsely chopped

½ tsp salt, or to taste

2 tsp garlic puree

2 tsp ginger puree

2 green chiles, coarsely chopped (seeded if you like)

1 cup coarsely chopped fresh cilantro, including the tender stalks

1 tsp garam masala

vegetable oil, for brushing

2 tbsp butter, melted

mint and spinach relish, to serve

Put the cashew nuts in a heatproof bowl, cover with boiling water, and let soak for 20 minutes. Drain and put in a food processor. Add the cream and egg and process the ingredients to a coarse mixture.

Add all the remaining ingredients, except the oil and melted butter, and process until smooth. Transfer to a bowl, cover, and let chill in the refrigerator for 30 minutes.

Preheat the broiler to high. Brush the broiler rack and 8 metal skewers lightly with oil. Have a bowl of cold water ready.

Divide the chilled mixture into 8 equal-size balls. Dip your hands into the bowl of cold water—this will stop the mixture from sticking to your fingers when you are molding it onto the skewers. Carefully mold each ball onto the skewers, patting and stretching it gently into a 6-inch/15-cm sausage shape. Arrange the kabobs on the prepared broiler rack and cook about 6 inches/15 cm below the heat source for 4 minutes. Brush with half the melted butter and cook for an additional 1 minute. Turn over and cook for 3 minutes. Baste with the remaining melted butter and cook for an additional 2 minutes.

Remove from the heat and let the kabobs rest for 5 minutes before sliding them off the skewers with a table knife. Serve with the relish.

meatballs with tomato relish

serves 4

1 onion, finely chopped

2 garlic cloves, finely chopped

2 slices bread, crusts removed

1 lb 2 oz/500 g lean ground beef

1 cooked baby beet, chopped

pinch of paprika

2 tsp finely chopped fresh thyme

1 egg

salt and pepper

fresh thyme sprigs, to garnish

tomato relish

⅓ cup strain, pureed tomatoes

2 tsp creamed horseradish

Preheat the oven to 450°F/230°C. To make the tomato relish, mix the strained tomatoes and creamed horseradish together in a small bowl. Cover and reserve until required.

Place the onion, garlic, and 2 teaspoons of water in a small saucepan and simmer over low heat for 5 minutes. Increase the heat, bring to a boil and cook until all the water has evaporated. Remove from the heat.

Meanwhile, tear the bread into pieces and place in a small bowl. Add enough cold water just to cover and let soak for 5 minutes. Squeeze the excess water from the bread and place in a bowl with the beef, onion-and-garlic mixture, beet, paprika, thyme, and egg. Season to taste with salt and pepper and mix thoroughly.

Form the mixture into 24 small balls between the palms of your hands. Thread 3 balls onto each of 8 skewers and place on a baking sheet. Bake in the preheated oven for 10 minutes, or until well browned. Transfer to a serving dish, garnish with a few sprigs of fresh thyme, and serve with the tomato relish.

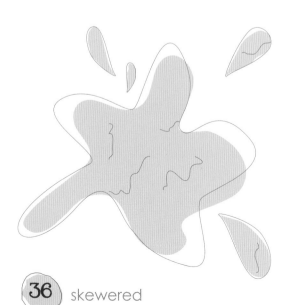

pork & peanut kabobs

serves 6

2 medium red onions

1 lb 2 oz/500 g ground pork

½ tsp chile flakes

⅓ cup chunky peanut butter

1 cup fresh white breadcrumbs

finely grated zest of ½ orange

salt and pepper

⅓ cup salted peanuts,
chopped, to sprinkle

salsa

1 orange

1 small red onion, finely diced

1 tbsp olive oil

Soak 6 bamboo skewers in cold water for 10 minutes.

Cut one of the onions into small wedges and put to one side. Very finely chop or grate the remaining onion, then place in a large bowl with the pork, chile flakes, peanut butter, breadcrumbs, orange zest, salt, and pepper.

Using your hands, mix the ingredients together thoroughly. Form into 24 small balls, about 1¾ inches/4.5 cm in diameter. Thread 4 balls onto each bamboo skewer with a wedge of onion at each end. Place on a baking sheet, cover, and chill for 10 minutes, or until required.

For the salsa, cut away all the peel and white pith from the orange, then remove the segments, catching the juice in a bowl. Coarsely chop the segments and add to the juices with the diced onion and olive oil.

Preheat a broiler to moderately hot. Cook the skewers on the baking sheet under the broiler for about 15 minutes, turning occasionally, until golden brown and thoroughly cooked.

Serve the meatballs sprinkled with the chopped peanuts, with the orange salsa on the side.

turkey & rosemary kabobs

serves 4

4 firm twigs of rosemary, about 10 inches/25 cm long

14 oz/400 g ground turkey

scant 1 cup rolled oats

1 medium red bell pepper, seeded and finely chopped

1 small onion, very finely chopped

½ tsp smoked paprika

salt and pepper

olive oil for brushing

Greek-style yogurt, to serve

salad greens, to serve

Snip the top 2 inches/5 cm of sprig from the rosemary and reserve. Strip the remaining leaves from the twigs and soak the stems in cold water for 10 minutes. Finely chop 1 tablespoon of the leaves.

Place the turkey, oats, bell pepper, onion, chopped rosemary, paprika, salt, and pepper in a bowl and mix together thoroughly with your hands. Shape into 16 small balls, about 2 inches/5 cm diameter. Thread 4 balls onto each rosemary twig. Place on a lightly greased baking sheet, cover, and chill for 10 minutes, or until required.

Preheat a broiler to moderately hot. Lightly brush the meatballs with oil and cook on the baking sheet under the broiler for 15–18 minutes, turning occasionally, until evenly browned and firm.

Press the reserved fresh sprigs of rosemary at one end of each skewer and serve hot with a spoonful of yogurt and fresh salad greens.

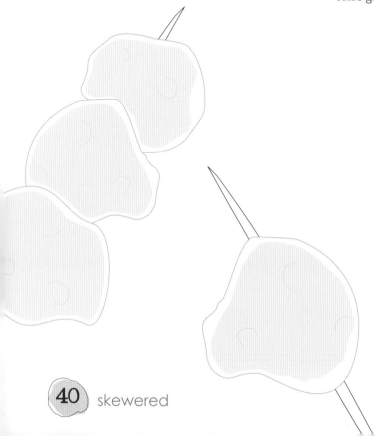

fish & coconut balls

serves 4

oil for greasing

3–4 lemongrass stalks

12 oz/350 g monkfish fillet, or other white fish

4 scallions, chopped

2 tsp Thai green curry paste

3½ oz/100 g peeled shrimp, chopped

4 tbsp coconut milk

1¼ cups fresh white breadcrumbs

sesame oil, for brushing

lime wedges, to serve

Preheat the oven to 400°F/200°C. Grease a baking sheet with oil. Cut the lemongrass stalks in quarters lengthwise, then cut into 3½-inch/9-cm lengths. Soak in cold water for 10 minutes.

Cut the monkfish into chunks and place in a food processor with the scallions and curry paste. Process for a few seconds to chop fairly finely, but keep coarse in texture; if the fish is chopped too finely, it will become mushy.

Stir in the shrimp, coconut milk, and breadcrumbs, mixing thoroughly. Shape the mixture into 12–14 balls and place on the baking sheet. Brush lightly with oil and skewer each ball with a lemongrass stalk.

Bake in the oven for 15–20 minutes, until golden brown and just firm. Serve warm, with lime wedges, as an appetizer.

Wrapped

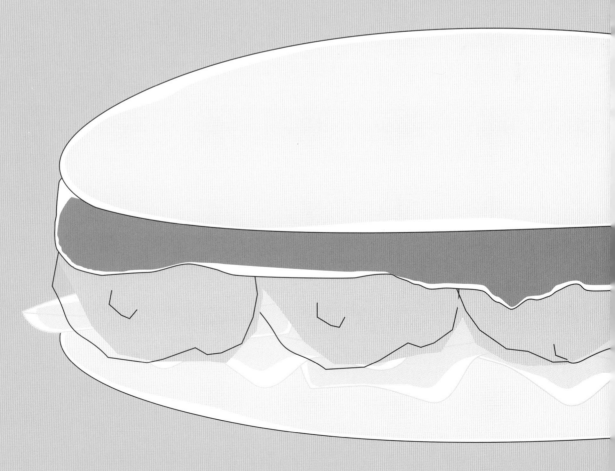

chicken meatball wrap

serves 4

14 oz/400 g chicken breast, diced

1 apple, coarsely grated

½ cup coarsely grated Cheddar cheese

1 cup fresh white breadcrumbs

2 tbsp chopped chives

salt and pepper

whole wheat flour, for dusting

oil, for shallow frying

4 whole wheat tortilla wraps

2½ oz/75 g watercress or argula leaves

Place the chicken in a food processor and process on "pulse" for a few seconds to chop finely. Mix the chicken with the apple, cheese, breadcrumbs, chives, salt, and pepper.

Shape the mixture into about 20 small balls and roll in flour to coat lightly. Chill for 10 minutes, or until required.

Heat a shallow depth of oil in a wok or heavy skillet and fry the chicken meatballs for 6–8 minutes, turning often, until golden brown and firm. Drain on absorbent paper towels.

Warm the tortilla wraps slightly, fold over to make pockets, and fill with watercress and the meatballs to serve. Wrap with a paper napkin to hold the wrap in place.

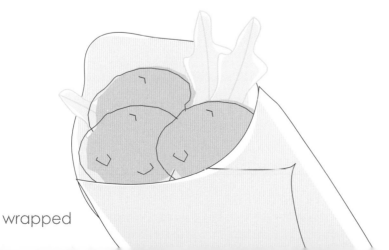

bacon-wrapped turkey meatballs

serves 4

1 lb 2 oz/500 g ground turkey

1 medium onion, finely chopped

⅔ cup finely chopped fresh or frozen cranberries

2 tbsp finely chopped sage leaves

salt and pepper

10 slices bacon or pancetta

cranberry sauce, to serve

Place the turkey, onion, cranberries, sage, salt, and pepper in a large bowl and mix thoroughly with your hands. Shape into about 20 small balls, 1½–2 inches/4–5 cm in diameter.

Place the bacon on a cutting board and press each slice with the back of a knife to stretch thinly. Cut in half across the middle and wrap each piece around a meatball. Place on a baking sheet, with the seam underneath, cover, and chill in the refrigerator for 10 minutes, or until required.

Preheat the oven to 400°F/200°C. Bake the meatballs on the baking sheet for 20–25 minutes, or until golden and firm.

Serve the meatballs hot with the cranberry sauce.

vegetarian eggplant balls

serves 4

2 large eggplants

olive oil, for brushing

1 medium red onion

2 cloves garlic, crushed

4 cups stale white breadcrumbs

1 cup finely grated
Parmesan cheese

2 egg yolks

3 tbsp chopped basil

salt and pepper

flour, for dusting

oil, for frying

4 corn tortilla wraps, warmed

sprigs of basil, to garnish

salsa

4 baby plum tomatoes, chopped

2 tsp red wine vinegar

1 tsp light brown sugar

1 tbsp capers, rinsed and
finely chopped

Preheat the oven to 400°F/200°C.

Halve the eggplants lengthwise, brush with oil, sprinkle with salt and pepper, and place, cut-side down on a baking sheet. Halve the onion, leaving on the skin, and place, cut-side down on the baking sheet. Roast in the oven for 20–25 minutes, until tender.

Scoop out the flesh from the eggplant and chop. Skin and finely chop the onion. Mix together the eggplant, onion, garlic, breadcrumbs, Parmesan, egg yolks, and basil. Season well with salt and pepper. Using lightly floured hands, shape the mixture into 20 balls. Chill for 10 minutes, or until needed.

For the salsa, combine all the ingredients, season to taste, and stir well.

Heat an 1-inch/2.5-cm depth of oil in a wok or deep pan and fry the eggplant balls in batches for 2–3 minutes, until golden brown, turning occasionally. Drain on absorbent paper towels.

Serve the balls in warmed corn tortilla wraps shaped into cones, with the tomato salsa and basil sprigs.

meatball hero

serves 4

1 lb/450 g lean ground beef

1 small onion, grated

2 cloves garlic, crushed

½ cup fine white breadcrumbs

1 tsp hot chili sauce

salt and pepper

whole wheat flour, for dusting

oil, for shallow frying

sandwich

1 tbsp olive oil

1 small onion, sliced

oblong rolls or small baguettes

4 tbsp mayonnaise

2 oz/55 g prepared
sliced jalapeños

2 tbsp mustard

Mix together the ground beef, onion, garlic, breadcrumbs, chili sauce, salt, and pepper. Shape into 20 small balls using floured hands. Cover and chill for 10 minutes, or until required.

Heat a shallow depth of oil in a wok or heavy skillet until very hot, then fry the meatballs in batches for 6–8 minutes, turning often, until golden brown and firm. Drain on absorbent paper towels and keep hot.

Heat the olive oil in a clean pan and fry the onions over moderate heat, stirring occasionally, until soft and golden brown.

Split the rolls lengthwise and spread with mayonnaise. Arrange the onions, meatballs, and jalapeños over the bottom half, squeeze the mustard over, and top with the other half. Serve the rolls immediately.

lamb & olive meatballs

serves 4-6

1 lb 2 oz/500 g lean ground lamb

1 medium onion, finely chopped

1 clove garlic, crushed

2 tbsp chopped mint

20 pitted black olives

10 sheets phyllo pastry

salt and pepper

olive oil, for brushing

Preheat the oven to 375°F/190°C.

Mix together the lamb, onion, garlic, and mint, then season well with salt and pepper. Divide into 20 equal pieces, then press each out to a round and place an olive in the center. Fold over the meat mixture to enclose the olives, pressing firmly together.

Cut the phyllo pastry to make 60 squares, measuring about 4½ inches/12 cm. Brush lightly with oil and stack in threes, offsetting the angles to make star shapes. Place a meatball on each and bring up the edges and press together to form a parcel.

Place the parcels on a baking sheet, brush with oil, and bake in the oven for about 20 minutes, until golden brown. Serve hot.

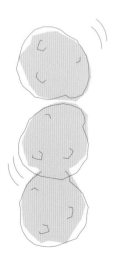

meatball marinara

serves 4

1 lb/450 g lean ground beef

1 medium onion, finely chopped

1 clove garlic, crushed

3 tbsp finely chopped parsley

1 small egg, beaten

salt and pepper

flour, for dusting

oil, for shallow frying

oblong rolls or small baguettes

marinara sauce

3 tbsp olive oil

1 small onion, chopped

2 cloves garlic, crushed

14 oz/400 g canned
chopped tomatoes

1 tbsp chopped oregano

½ tsp superfine sugar

To make the meatballs, thoroughly mix together the beef, onion, garlic, parsley, egg, salt, and pepper. Shape into about 20 small balls with lightly floured hands. Cover and chill until required.

For the sauce, heat the oil in a wide saucepan and fry the onion and garlic over moderate heat for about 10 minutes, stirring often, until softened but not browned. Stir in the tomatoes, oregano, sugar, salt, and pepper. Cover and simmer gently for 20 minutes, stirring occasionally, until no free liquid remains.

Heat a shallow depth of oil in a wok or heavy skillet and fry the meatballs over moderate heat for 8–10 minutes, until firm and golden brown. Drain on absorbent paper towels.

Split the rolls lengthwise. Arrange the meatballs over the bottom half, spoon over the marinara sauce, and top with the other half. Serve immediately.

meatball calzone

serves 4
dough

3 cups white bread flour, plus
extra for dusting

1tsp salt

1 sachet fast action yeast

1¼ cups warm water

1 tbsp olive oil, plus
extra for greasing

1 tbsp milk, for brushing

filling

1 medium onion

14 oz/400 g ground pork

2 tbsp finely chopped parsley

1 clove garlic, crushed

2 tbsp olive oil

4 plum tomatoes, chopped

1 tbsp tomato paste

1 tsp dried oregano

3½ oz/100 g mozzarella, chopped

salt and pepper

Combine the flour, salt, and yeast in a bowl, add the water and oil, and mix to a soft dough. Turn out and knead for 6–8 minutes, until smooth. Cover and let stand in a warm place for about 1 hour, until doubled in size.

For the filling, finely chop half the onion and mix with the pork, parsley, garlic, salt, and pepper. Shape into 20 small balls. Heat 1 tablespoon of oil in a wok or skillet and fry the meatballs in batches for 5–6 minutes, turning often, until golden brown and firm. Drain on absorbent paper towels.

Thinly slice the remaining half of onion and fry in the remaining oil for 2–3 minutes, until softened. Add the tomatoes, tomato paste, oregano, salt, and pepper and cook over moderate heat, stirring occasionally, for 6–8 minutes, until reduced to a thick pulp.

Preheat the oven to 425°F/220°C. Lightly oil 2 baking sheets.

Knead the dough briefly, then divide into 4 and roll each to an 8-inch/20-cm round. Spread the tomato mixture on one side of each, within ¾ inch/2 cm of the edge. Top with the meatballs and mozzarella.

Brush the edges of the dough with milk and fold over to enclose the filling, tucking and pinching the edges to seal. Lift onto the baking sheets, cover, and let rest for 10 minutes.

Brush with milk and pierce a hole to release steam, then bake in the oven for 15–20 minutes, until crisp and golden. Serve hot.

ham corn meatballs

serves 4

1 lb/450 g lean unsmoked ham

1 medium onion, quartered

7 oz/200 g canned corn
kernels, drained

3 tbsp fine polenta or cornmeal

salt and pepper

oil for deep-frying

lemon wedges, to serve

batter

¾ cup all-purpose flour

1 tsp mild chili powder

1 egg, beaten

scant ½ cup mixed milk and water

Cut the ham into chunks, place in a food processor, and process on "pulse" for several seconds, until finely chopped. Turn into a large bowl.

Finely chop the onion in the food processor and add to the bowl. Roughly process the corn kernels on "pulse" for a few seconds and add to the bowl. Stir in the polenta and season lightly with salt and pepper. Shape into 16 small balls, cover, and chill until required.

For the batter, place all the ingredients in the food processor and process until smooth and bubbly.

Heat a deep pan of oil to 350°F/180°C, or until a cube of bread browns in 30 seconds. Dip each meatball in the batter, drain off the excess, and lower into the hot oil. Fry in batches for about 6 minutes each, turning often, until golden brown. Drain on absorbent paper towels.

Serve the meatballs immediately, with lemon wedges.

Chilled

chicken & ginger meatballs

serves 4

1 lb 2 oz/500 g skinless, boneless chicken thighs

4 scallions, roughly chopped

1-inch/2.5-cm piece fresh ginger, grated

⅓ cup coarsely chopped cilantro

salt and pepper

cornstarch, for dusting

sesame oil, for greasing

sweet chili sauce or soy sauce, to serve

shredded vegetable salad, to serve

Trim any excess fat from the chicken, then place in a food processor with the scallions, ginger, cilantro, salt, and pepper. Process in short bursts until finely chopped but still with some texture.

Lightly dust your hands with cornstarch and roll the mixture into 18–20 small balls. Cover and chill until required.

Pour boiling water into a steamer and bring to a boil. Brush the steamer basket with sesame oil, then add the meatballs, cover, and steam for 12–15 minutes, until firm.

Drain the meatballs, cool completely, then chill before serving. Serve with the sweet chili sauce or soy sauce for dipping and with a finely shredded vegetable salad.

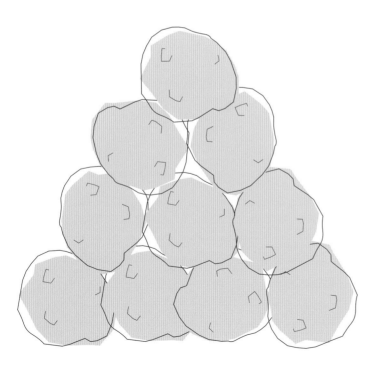

turkey meatballs

serves 4

1½ medium zucchini

3 large shallots, grated

1 lb/450 g ground turkey

½ cup dry white breadcrumbs

½ tsp grated nutmeg

salt and pepper

oil, for shallow frying

sesame seeds, for coating

cherry tomatoes and carrot sticks,
for serving

Grate the zucchini on a fairly fine grater, or grate in a food processor. Place in a strainer and press out any excess liquid. Mix with the shallots, turkey, breadcrumbs, nutmeg, salt, and pepper.

Shape the mixture with your hands into 24 small balls. Cover and chill until required.

Heat about a ½-inch/1-cm depth of oil in a wok or heavy skillet until a piece of mixture sizzles immediately. Fry the meatballs in batches on a moderate heat for 10–12 minutes, turning often, until golden brown and firm.

Drain the meatballs on absorbent paper towels, then quickly toss in sesame seeds to coat lightly. Cool completely, then chill and serve cold with cherry tomatoes and carrot sticks.

turkey & spinach meatballs

serves 4

1 cup cooked young spinach,
fresh or frozen

1 lb 2 oz/500 g ground turkey

2½ oz/70 g feta cheese

1 large egg, beaten

1½ cups fresh white breadcrumbs

salt and pepper

oil, for frying

Place the spinach in a strainer and use a wooden spoon to press out as much moisture as possible. Chop coarsely with a sharp knife. Mix together the spinach and turkey and season well with salt and pepper.

Cut the feta cheese into 16 small chunks. Divide the meat mixture into 16 and shape around the feta to form small balls, enclosing the cheese completely. Chill for 10 minutes, or until required.

Dip the meatballs in beaten egg to coat lightly, then roll in breadcrumbs to coat evenly.

Heat about a 1-inch/2.5-cm depth of oil in a wok or deep skillet and fry the meatballs, turning often, for 8–10 minutes, or until golden brown and firm. Drain on absorbent paper towels.

Let cool before serving. The meatballs make a good picnic or lunch box treat.

beef & pecan meatballs

serves 4

1 lb 2 oz/500 g lean ground beef

1 small onion, finely chopped

½ cup finely chopped pecans

2 tbsp Dijon mustard

2 tbsp maple syrup

1 tbsp olive oil

salt and pepper

20 pecan halves

Boston lettuce, to serve

Preheat the oven to 400°F/200°C.

Mix together the ground beef, onion, and pecans, and season to taste with salt and pepper. Shape the mixture into about 20 small balls, pressing a pecan half into the top of each. Place on a baking sheet.

Mix together the mustard, maple syrup, and oil and brush over the meatballs. Bake in the oven for about 15 minutes, until golden brown and firm.

Cool before serving in the lettuce, placing each on a small leaf to serve as a canapé, or serve in groups on larger leaves for an appetizer.

pork meatballs

serves 4

oil, for greasing

1 lb 2 oz/500 g ground pork

1 medium onion, grated

1 cup finely chopped dried apricots

1 tbsp Worcestershire sauce

salt and pepper

1 small egg, beaten

¾ cup pine nuts

Preheat the oven to 350°F/180°C. Lightly grease a baking sheet.

Thoroughly mix together the pork, onion, apricots, and Worcestershire sauce, and season with salt and pepper. Shape into 24 small balls with your hands.

Dip the meatballs quickly into the beaten egg, then press into the pine nuts to coat the tops. Place on the baking sheet.

Bake the meatballs in the oven for about 15 minutes, until firm and golden brown. Cool completely, then cool and chill until required.

salmon sushi balls

serves 6-8

2 cups short-grain rice

2½ cups water

2 tbsp rice vinegar

2 tsp superfine sugar

1 tsp salt

2 tsp grated fresh ginger

5½ oz/150 g sliced
smoked salmon

sprigs of fresh dill, to garnish

wasabi, to serve

Wash the rice thoroughly under cold running water, and then drain well.

Place the rice in a heavy-bottom pan with the water, cover, and bring to a boil. Let simmer on moderate heat for 10 minutes. Reduce the heat to low and let simmer for an additional 5 minutes. Remove from the heat and let stand to cool, still covered.

Mix together the vinegar, sugar, salt, and ginger, then stir through the rice. Shape the rice into about 30 small balls.

Cut the salmon into 1¼–1½-inch/3–4-cm squares. Place a sprig of dill onto a 6-inch/15-cm square of plastic wrap, top with a square of salmon and a rice ball, gather up the edges of the plastic, and twist to make a firm ball. Repeat to make about 30 balls, and chill in the refrigerator for at least 20 minutes.

Unwrap the rice balls and serve cold as a canapé or appetizer, with a dab of wasabi on the side.

crabmeat balls

serves 4

1 cup finely crushed matzo crackers or cheese crackers

7 oz/200 g dressed crabmeat (white and dark)

1 egg white

4 scallions, very finely chopped

1 small red chile, seeded and finely chopped

juice of ½ lime

Preheat the oven to 425°F/ 220°C.

Reserve ¼ cup of the cracker crumbs and mix the rest with the crabmeat, egg white, scallions, chile, and lime juice. Mix to a firm mixture, adding an extra squeeze of lime juice, if necessary, to bind.

Divide the mixture into 16 and roll into walnut-size balls. Roll in the reserved cracker crumbs to coat lightly and arrange on a baking sheet.

Bake the crabmeat balls in the oven for about 10 minutes, until lightly browned and crisp. Cool before serving as a canapé, or with salad greens for an appetizer.

mushroom & bean balls

serves 4-6

12 oz/350 g cup smushrooms, quartered

1 small onion, quartered

15 oz/425 g canned red kidney beans, rinsed and drained thoroughly

1 clove garlic, crushed

1 tbsp chopped thyme

1 small egg, beaten

1½ cups fresh whole wheat breadcrumbs

salt and pepper

whole wheat flour, for dusting

oil, for shallow frying

avocado dip

1 ripe avocado

juice of 1 small lemon

1 tsp chopped thyme

Place the mushrooms and onion in a food processor and process until finely chopped. Add the beans, garlic, thyme, egg, and breadcrumbs and process in short bursts until the mixture just binds together. Season with salt and pepper.

Shape the mixture into about 20 small balls, using lightly floured hands. Heat a ½-inch/1-cm depth of oil in a wok or heavy skillet and fry the balls, turning often, until golden brown. Drain on absorbent paper towels, and let cool.

Puree the avocado flesh with the lemon juice and thyme, season to taste, and serve with the mushroom balls.